MW01675308

WHAT REVIEV

"If you don't have 1 million dollars, this book is indispensable for global gypsies. It'll probably save you so much money with your travel, you'll wind up a millionaire."

Robin Leach
Host of LIFESTYLES OF THE RICH AND FAMOUS

"Hubbell has compiled practical advice in an easy-to-read style. The "Definitely Worthwhile" segment recommends many worthwhile places to visit in the United States, while "50 Nifty Car Games" will prove useful regardless whether the drive is cross country or crosstown."

Library Journal

"In a tough economy here's a book filled with tips on how to get the maximum enjoyment from your vacation with a minimum expense."

Book Views (Alan Caruba)

"Emphasis is on affordable domestic touring: her famiy oriented guide achieves this goal by providing a simple game plan for planning and organizing trips, from location bargains to reducing travel related stress."

The Bookwatch

"If you like to travel, you will love this book! It's an original to be sure and includes essential info. Don't Miss this one!

Families Together

"Designed for families but informative for all travelers, it provides basic travel rules in an organized, humorous, and easy-to-read handbook."

The Bloomsbury Review

LUXURY TRAVEL FOR THE UNRICH AND UNFAMOUS

How To See The USA In An Affordable Way

A Family Guidebook

by

Beth Hubbell

Illustrations by Jim Patten
Cover Art by Betty Hagberg

Second Edition

Jeremiah Publications, Haslett Michigan

LUXURY TRAVEL FOR THE UNRICH AND UNFAMOUS

How To See The USA In An Affordable Way

A Family Guidebook

Beth Hubbell

Second Printing

Library of Congress Catalog Card Number: 91-75576

ISBN: 0-9631131-6-x

by Jeremiah Publications
1158 Woodside Dr. #102
Haslett, MI 48840

Illustrations by Jim Patten
Cover Art by Betty Hagberg
Editorial Assistance by Gayle Harris

Printed in the United States of America

To my Parents
who inspired my traveling instincts
And to my Family
without whom these ideas
could never have been perfected
And especially
to Dick H.

About the Author

Beth Hubbell, is a former teacher and seasoned traveler, having visited almost every state as well as parts of Canada and Europe. She has traveled both on her own and with her family, utilizing almost every mode of transportation available, from water taxi to jumbo jet. During her many journeys, she has perfected the art of saving money when possible so that important experiences and adventures don't have to be missed. She offers this wealth of information to you, saving you the Trial & Error Method.

TABLE OF CONTENTS

INTRODUCTION

Tired of finding campgrounds with no vacancies, pitching tents in the rain, keeping track of wandering children, cooking over fires that won't start? If you're not a Happy Camper, but still want to see the USA (Canada too) without having to mortgage your house, you can not only save money but also time, when you leave your tent at home. Sounds like you're ready for LUXURY TRAVEL—on a budget, of course. Think about it—real beds, clean sheets, swimming pools, and Putt Putts! Ready to pack your bags? Read on. At last a book about how YOU the average unrich, unfamous American family can enjoy the luxury of Motel

Travel! Yes, we're talking motels, hotels, Red Roofs, or roofs of any color, for that matter, as long as they're not canvas!

Now for all you single parents and others who think you're not included, the definition of family in this case is: one or more people who can stand being in the same close proximity for hours at a time (Quality Time!). So take Grandma, Grandpa, or a friend (with or without kids)—not only will it help you keep your sanity, but it should give you an occasional break from the kids and possibly some driving relief (remember adult conversations?).

Even for the most avid of campers, camping isn't always the most practical way to go. In fact, believe it or not, there are actually some drawbacks. Keep these in mind in case you need to rationalize about this alternate style of travel to yourself, your spouse, your kids, or whomever else needs convincing.

CAMPING—YOU MUST BE KIDDING!

Yes, there are limits to camping. Consider cities for instance. How many campgrounds are located in the city of Washington, D.C., Chicago, San Francisco, New York, or Los Angeles? Let's face it, most campgrounds are going to be on the outskirts of town. Ask yourself what attractions you might want to see if you were visiting one of those cities. Chances are you're going to want to do your sightseeing mainly in town. The further out you stay from these areas, the more time you will spend fighting the traffic going back and forth, plus the extra time (not to mention work) it takes to set up and take down your camp. You will also have the extra expenses of gas and parking fees OR the costs of public transportation if it is available. So even if camping usually works for you, in cases like these you may want to opt for a hotel in town.

Of course you'll want to consider the security element and public transportation routes, as well as the location of places you wish to visit in choosing your hotel. But you may be surprised at the nice accommodations you can find, and staying in town is a great way to feel the real charm of the city! If hotel rates seem high, be sure to subtract the extra costs mentioned above (gas, parking, public transportation) which you will now be saving, before making your decision. With the extra time you gain, you will be able to include more in your itinerary or just use it for relaxing and enjoying all the comforts your hotel has to offer. You'll be glad you eliminated the extra stress of driving in an unfamiliar city!

RENTING A RECREATION VEHICLE
Look Before You Leap!

Renting an RV is another popular method of family travel, because they are generally more comfortable and belongings are more easily accessible. However, this set-up has many of the same drawbacks as tent accommodations, such as finding convenient campsites. You may save time on set up and clean up depending on the design of your vehicle, but you may lose that time trying to find parking everywhere you go if your rig is larger than a standard van. Also if you plan to do much driving, RVs can be real gas guzzlers. If you don't already own one, checking around for rental fees may be enough to convince you that camping with an RV may not be your best option either. In fact, even though camping in general can be a great family vacation, sometimes it's just not practical when you really want to cover territory and see the sights! Time is a premium for 90's families—often trying to juggle two work schedules and various kids' activities. Extra stress on your vacation is something you don't need!

THE WAY TO GO!
Five Basic Rules To Follow

How's the motel idea sounding now? Don't pack your bags yet. **PLANNING AHEAD** is the real key to the success of your trip (more about that in Chapter 1), and the following basic guidelines will help to keep you on track. If you are already putting some of these into practice, you are definitely headed in the right direction.

1. **Eat only one meal out a day** (You'll not only save time but also eat better for less).

2. **Set an average daily limit on spending.** The American Automobile Association recommends that a family of four, vacationing by car should budget $50 a day per person; however, with this plan we have been able to do it for half that – $100 a day has been a workable goal for our family of four (personal spending not included). You will need to adjust your goal according to your family's size and any current economic crises, particularly relating to gasoline prices, and also, if you go to California, New York City, or other high cost areas. Keep records; often if you have to go over the limit one day, you can make up for it by cutting back on another day.
3. **Always visit tourist attractions early** (Beat the Crowds)!
4. **Make Hotel/Motel Reservations far in advance** (Gain Travel Time & Save Big Bucks).
5. **Make the most of what you already have** (Recycle when you can, and although more difficult when traveling, always be on the lookout for other ways to conserve our natural resources).

Read on to learn how these Five Basic Rules can help your family enjoy great vacations without going hopelessly into debt.

CHAPTER 1

PLANNING AHEAD
What A Concept!

Although a good travel plan requires considerable planning time, it is also part of the fun. This is the time for ideas and dreams to be shared by all members of the family before the realities of actual travel enter in. However, before bringing THE TRIP up for open discussion, it's a good idea for parents to do their homework. There are really two planning phases. The first is the LONG TERM PLAN and the second is the INDIVIDUAL TRIP PLAN.

THE LONG TERM PLAN
Down The Road

This plan is geared to map out individual trip plans for the coming years. It covers the years your children are at suitable ages for the kind of travel you wish to do. Obviously if you don't mind hiking with a baby on your back or if you have only a couple of children fairly close in age, you will have more years available for prime travel time. However, my recommendation would be that if you do have very young children, plan a "Stay In One Place Vacation" like renting a campsite or cottage (You can always take sidetrips to interesting places in the area). Save the traveling vacations until the children are not only old enough to help, but can gain more educationally.

Start with a brainstorming session where you write down all the places you would like to share with your children. This should include any long lost friends or relatives you may wish to visit. Then group your list into areas fairly close in proximity such as the Washington, D.C. area which might also cover Baltimore & other places on the Chesapeake Bay, or parts of Pennsylvania like Gettysburg, Hershey, or the Amish country and various store outlets around Lancaster. Lastly and most importantly, you will need to match these groupings to the interest levels of your children. If your children cover a wide age range, this will be more difficult as many attractions don't appeal to all ages. For each area try to come up with some things that all of you can enjoy together; then add at least one other attraction, something special for each child. Sometimes it is necessary to divide up to keep everyone happy—like at Cedar Point Amusement Park where not everyone can handle trying to set a record for the most roller coaster rides!

You should end up with some sort of chart for your Long Term Plan, which begins with the year your youngest child will first be old enough to travel and end the year before your oldest child will be getting a job or refuses to be seen in public with his family (this is usually about the same time—age 15 is about the most you can hope for). If your family's age range is too broad, you may sometimes need to leave part of your family elsewhere. Friends with children close to the same age as yours, grandparents, or other relatives have been known to come to the rescue in cases like these.

Find the most appropriate year for each of your proposed trips and add them to the chart, starting with a short excursion (2–4 days) like maybe Sea World or some other attraction close to home combined with a visit to a friend's or relative's place, and ending with your most extensive trip like one to the opposite end of the country which requires considerably more travel time. Any years for which you have no travel plans or just a short trip, add a "Stay In One Place Vacation" such as: a camping trip, a boating excursion, renting a cottage or condo at a beach, or if you can afford it, try one of the many specialized resorts or adventure vacations where everything is organized for you and babysitting is available. For example: Club Med offers beautiful resort areas—some geared to families. Dress in these resorts is very casual, rooms quite basic, and there are lots of activities from which to choose.

Our master plan from our Michigan location looked like the chart on the following page.

With your master plan, you can still be flexible—deciding what time of year will be best for your various vacations and, of course, making changes when new opportunities arise. But, if you keep the total picture in mind, you won't find yourself suffering from the "if onlys" when your childrens' friends become more important and they no longer want to travel with their parents—inevitably sooner than you might think!

THE INDIVIDUAL TRIP PLAN
Doing It YOUR Way!

The second planning phase is the INDIVIDUAL TRIP PLAN, a guide to be used for planning the various trips within your LONG TERM PLAN as it becomes time for them. This plan is recommended with even the simplist of trips, because it is a major way to keep expenses down and also not miss anything important. The deals are out there, but they go fast! The key here is information—the more the better! So if possible, at least 3–9 months ahead of your

LONG TERM 10 YEAR PLAN

Year	Place	Mode of Travel	Length of Trip	Other Vacations	Kids' Ages
1980	Sea World & Relatives	station wagon	4 days	cottage	4,6,14
1981	Florida	plane	5 days	camping	5,7,15
1982	Lake St. Clair	sailboat	4 days	cottage	6&8
1983	Chicago	train	3 days	camping	7,9,17
1984	Lake Michigan	sailboat	5 days	cottage	8&10
1985	Toronto-Boston	car	1 week	camping	9&11
1986	Beaver Island	sailboat	1 week	cottage	10&12
1987	Washington, D.C.	car	1 week	cottage	11&13
1988	Chesapeake Bay	sailboat	1 week	cottage	12&14
1989	Best of the West	minivan	3 weeks	-	13&15

scheduled trip (depending on where you plan to go), gather as much as you can. Join a Travel Club for maps and general information, get books, talk to friends, write or call the Chamber of Commerce or Tourist Bureau for specific tourist areas, get the listings from motel chains, Bed and Breakfasts if you're interested, and anyone over 50 can join the American Association of Retired Persons (AARP) for special discounts! Then dig out all the magazine articles and newspaper clippings that you've stashed away over the years (because you knew that someday you'd get there one way or another) and pull out the ones that might fit into your upcoming trip. These may include addresses to which you may write for additional information. And finally, get some books from the library about the areas you will be visiting that are age appropriate for your children, and also a Road Atlas or puzzle map that they can enjoy.

Now that you have enough information to thoroughly carpet your floor, you can get on with your planning. Instead of dreading this stage of planning, set aside an afternoon or evening to have fun with it. Keeping the appropriate maps handy, come up with your Must See list for the area you have chosen and your available time frame. Keep in mind various goals—education, fun, etc. Then make a list of interesting options that could be worked into your proposed route. At this point bring in your kids and share your plans with them. Let them look through any of the materials, sharing their own ideas and dreams.

Based on their interests, you will be able to tell which of the options you should try to include. Then using your maps and a mileage gauge, if you can find one, decide on a workable route—figuring in ample time for tourist stops, travel time, and the unexpected.

Write down possible places for your overnight stays. Try to schedule major tourist attractions so that you arrive early to help avoid the crowds (very important)! Check your travel and motel guides to see what lodging is available near the locations chosen. Call to find out the best deal for the money, (many of these places have 800 numbers so it won't cost you anything). Take your family's needs into consideration: will they need to have something to do like swimming? will you need a laundry, etc.? Be sure to plan for daily fresh air and exercise. That, along with nutritious food, will help keep all your travelers healthy and happy. Shop around, ask questions, then reserve the best deal **Right Away**. Reserving your room by credit card for "late arrival" will make sure you don't arrive in Trails End, Montana late in the evening with exhausted children, your room only held 'til 6:00 P.M., and "No Vacancy" signs everywhere. Should your plans change, you can still cancel your reservation, often as late as 5:00 P.M., on your date of arrival, with no charge to you.

Planning and reserving your lodging ahead of time can save as much as a third of your lodging costs. You will be surprised at how many discounts are available; your travel club (AAA, Amoco, etc.) will be valuable in helping you here. Also many motel chains (Holiday Inn Priority Club, Super 8's VIP Membership, etc.) offer discounts (more about this in Chapter 4). Even where discounts are not available, you'll still be able to shop for the best rate for the type of motel you want.

All this can be a rather time consuming task, especially if you're planning an extensive trip. But it will be worth it later because you will gain considerable travel time and greatly ease the anxiety of entering a strange area each evening, hoping you can find some acceptable place to stay at a reasonable price often when everyone is tired and irritable. AND, it will give all of you the fun of imagining what your new home away from home will be like from the description in the travel guide! Also important, you will be able to leave an itinerary with friends or relatives who may need to get in touch with you in the event of an emergency.

Should you plan (and I hope you will) to stay at lodges or cabins in the National Parks, you should reserve at least six months in advance. Staying in the parks is great for many reasons, including:

- being able to take advantage of special educational programs led by the Rangers
- saving travel time and costs; thus, having more time to explore and enjoy the park—a great place to get your daily exercise

Our experience has been that the National Park lodging facilities, (including cafeterias, gift shops, etc.) are very well run, friendly, and relatively inexpensive.

Having carried out these initial planning stages, you and your family are free to relax and enjoy the coming weeks in anticipation of the fun and excitement you will experience on your vacation. Leave a few books, maps, and pamphlets around to keep the interest up, and be on the alert for any new information you may run across—special restaurants, etc. You may also find information that pertains to one of the other trips you have scheduled in your Long Term Plan; be sure to file it away in a safe place as it won't be long until you'll be needing that too!

CHAPTER 2
WHAT TO TAKE
a list of Lists!

When your trip is only a few weeks away, it's time to really get organized and talk about the basic essentials—food, clothing, etc.! If you've never been a list person, all that's about to change—you don't want to forget anything you might need for your "luxury" vacation. After all, if you wanted to rough it, all you'd need are your jeans, a sweatshirt, and your sleeping bag!

The reason for list making is understandable. The average brain can only store so much information for instant recall, and who wants to spend their whole vacation trying to think anyway. There's plenty of time for that when your expressway splits and you're completely engulfed by cars and semi-trucks all driving like they're on their way to a fire, and you're just trying to remember basically where you're going and how you're going to make it across three lanes of traffic in the next two seconds! Not only do you need to remember to bring things with you, but you also need to remember to repack them every time you stop. So in order to get started in the right direction, here's the LIST OF LISTS you'll need to make.

I. MAIN SURVIVAL ITEMS "I need the map, NOW!"

These are the things that must be readily available as you will discover before you are on the road for very long. Lists and suggestions for how to make the best use of these items will be covered later in this chapter.

Cooler—small but tall (try to find one that will fit inside your car instead of being relegated to the trunk)

Plastic Drink Container—small but tall (must fit in cooler)
—primary function is to hold ice & keep food from swimming in melted water

—can double as temporary drink container
—in an emergency (your thermos runs out) you can drink the ice water

Food & Snack Box—sturdy cardboard, large enough to hold small sizes of non-perishable food & snacks, small enough to fit in your car

Paper Products Bag—this can just be a plastic bag that groceries were bagged in at the store or something similar; used to hold your paper products like paper plates, plastic silverware, & various reusable bags that you will accumulate during the course of your trip. (see Food List later in this chapter)

Thermos Jug—1 gallon—this is your main drinking source so keep it relatively full of ice water (water is better for everyone than sugared drinks and no need to worry if it spills). Plenty of opportunities for other drinks elsewhere.

Maps, Travel Information, Lists (including itinerary & any reservation confirmations), a small Notebook for keeping a record of expenses, and of course, this Book—organize in envelopes or flat bags by areas to be traveled. Keep appropriate ones stored near navigator to be used as needed.

Purse—be sure to check your supplies of the usual essentials: tissues, Tylenol, local map or info, small snacks, & necessary kid things.

Cash, Travelers Checks, & a major Credit Card—a combination of these will provide you with maximum flexibility & security. Carrying a lot of cash is risky, so charge whenever you can. A few personal checks are handy to have for emergencies. It's best to keep these items in different locations, so if your wallet or purse is stolen, you won't be completely helpless. If necessary, you can have money wired through Western Union.

II. MISCELLANEOUS ESSENTIALS LIST "Where's the Toothpaste?"

This list is pretty much self-explanatory, but generally these are the items that make the difference between a comfortable, enjoyable trip, and miserable chaos!

Frequently Used Items—might be needed several times during the day

* General—

- lap tray—this is an amazingly versatile item (get the kind with legs that fold up or no legs for easy storage). Among it's limitless uses:
  - —your counter for preparing sandwiches & other lunch items
  - —surface for writing, drawing, coloring—pencils, etc. won't roll off
  - —game board, even cards!
  - —puzzle board
  - —roadway for small cars & trucks
- camera & plenty of film (buy at home, expensive to buy at tourist stops)
- tape recorder (even if your car has a tape deck)
- Goody Bag—to keep your sanity when all else seems to fail. Stash a **few** small extra interesting things-to-do items here for when everyone is tired and irritable—hopefully you won't need this at the beginning of your trip. Suggestions:
  - —tapes—should be appropriate for the ages of your travelers and can include: special music, comedy routines such as Bill Cosby or Bob Newhart, stories, special family recordings, and a blank for your own recording sessions
  - —comic books
  - —trivia games or books
  - —stickers to give kids for their log books

(one sticker for every hundred miles) see Ch.4
- small new toys or books for young children
- hand & finger puppets
- sewing cards
- magnetic games
- Etch-a-Sketch
- deck of cards
- colorforms – I understand that they will stick to car windows

• tissues & wet wipes
• first aid kit – this should already be in your car! (include Tylenol and/or Aspirin)
• flashlight
• sun screen
• bug spray
• binoculars

* Personal –
    • pillows – one for each kid
    • Things To Do Bag – some type of bag like a school bag for each kid, where they can pack some of their own special things they like to do. Let them come up with some of their own ideas, but do include items from all areas listed below – little ones will need more guidance; teenagers will undoubtedly have their own ideas for their "survival kit" like their walkman & tapes, candy (not chocolate, I hope, since it melts), change for

soda pop & video machines, etc. —no need to encourage them!

- —reading material
- —writing material: a log booklet (see Ch.4), a pad of plain paper, a list of names & addresses of friends, markers or colored pencils (crayons melt!), etc.
- —small games & puzzles
- —small toys, if desired (young ones usually need a favorite stuffed animal or doll)

- hats (for the sun)
- sweaters or sweatshirts
- drink cups—preferably plastic, a different color or design for each person so all can keep track of own cups; plastic cup holders if your car doesn't have them (see Ch. 3)

Seldom Used Items—needed once per day or less

* General—
  - coats
  - extra pair shoes
  - raingear for each (plastic ponchos take up very little room)
  - 1 umbrella
  - small plastic tablecloth
  - towels—for beach only
  - laundry detergent, dish detergent (sponge with attached detergent tube kept in plastic bag works well for dishes)
  - winter emergency gear (seasonal)—include

hats & warm clothing for all, a blanket, work gloves, ice scraper & snow brush, shovel, booster cables, warning light or road flares, kitty litter for traction

* Personal–

- suitcase **or** clothing duffle bag–1 per person
- sleeping bags–if needed for kids
- tote bag–this should be a lightweight, fairly roomy bag, preferably with a shoulder strap & various compartments to keep things organized; use instead of purse to carry what your family will need on day trips when you won't have easy access to your car (can be left in trunk when not needed; purse can also be left in trunk, but in the case of a van or wagon, be sure it's out of sight and all doors locked). Include needed items such as: local map & info, items from purse, camera & film (unless you have separate carrying case), small snacks & kid stuff, tablecloth & lunch items if desired
- shampoo, mirror, shaver, hairdryer, curling iron, etc. (whatever it takes to get beautiful)
- laundry bag–any large plastic bag will do

III. THE CLOTHING LIST mix or match?

This list should be a basic list that will apply to everyone in the family. Although you will need clothes for all kinds of weather, and an outfit or two that looks presentable in a restaurant, try to pack conservatively. Casual wear is always acceptable for tourists, so unless you're headed for the Metropolitan Opera or other such place, leave the fancy clothes at home. In the summer white pants or skirts go anywhere! During other seasons, you can go with any plain dark basic color. A good way to avoid excess baggage is to have a clothing suitcase or bag for each member of the family, which they are responsible for carrying. You should be able to carry enough clothes for up to a week or 10 days without having to do laundry. Parents should try to share a large suitcase (divided ones work great) so you can take another bag for your personal miscellaneous items like the hairdryer, etc. without cheating on the rules (one bag per person, remember?).

Sample Clothing List:

- long pants—1 good, 1 not
- shorts
- shirts—assorted, short sleeves
- good outfit (dress or skirt optional)
- underwear
- socks
- sweatshirts—1 good, 1 not

- light sweater or jacket
- sleepwear – 1 cool, 1 warmer
- swim suit
- belt – optional
- comfortable walking shoes, dress shoes or sandals if desired
- personal necessities – any required medication, hair items, jewelry, sunglasses, etc.

The above list is for summer, when most people do their traveling. To modify it for winter travel, simply eliminate the shorts and add a few warmer items. Listed earlier, the following clothes can be collected in bulk to be stored in various plastic bags (label if desired) in the back of your vehicle to be pulled out at appropriate times: raingear, extra shoes, towels for the beach, warm coats and winter gear when applicable.

Clothing Tips:

* **Each person should pack with a couple of different color themes in mind so that maximum combinations can be made from minimum items.**
* **Layer clothing so that you can easily adjust to the different temperatures you will experience.**

IV. THE FOOD LIST—be resourceful

You will mainly be preparing your own breakfasts and lunches so keep that in mind as you look through your cupboards for the basic staples. When making this list, consider what most members of the family will eat, the length of your trip, and the fact that your storage space will be at a premium—this is no time for idiosyncrasies. Continue your list by taking a look through your refrigerator, being even more selective. Write down only those items that will be part of your basic food plan or that you can use up in the first couple of days. Indicate these refrigerator items with an "R" or other identifying mark. This will allow you to assess how well your "R"s will fit into your cooler and will aid you when it is time to pack. Add to your list any snacks (nutritious if possible), paper products, and items you will need to purchase before you leave. When it comes to actually packing (this is a good time to clean out your cupboard), throw in all the odds and ends you bought because your kids just had to have them, but never ate. When they're desperate, as they will be in the car, they'll eat practically anything!

Sample Food List:
For the **Cooler**–

- orange (or other) juice–2 days worth (we buy 1 qt.), if you buy a can of concentrate, remember you'll need an appropriate container to mix it in and you'll have to wash it–more work & time!
- milk–2 days worth (1 qt. works for us)
- sandwich meat & cheese–2 days worth
- fruit–washed
- carrots & celery–prepare ahead & store in plastic bag

** Optional–jelly (to go with peanut butter), hard boiled eggs (should be used the 1st or 2nd day for breakfast or lunch)

For the **Food and Snack Box**–

- bread
- peanut butter
- Keep several of the following non-perishables on hand in small sizes: raisins or other dried fruit, crackers, cookies (fig or other newtons and/or other non-chocolate varieties), chips or other munchies, granola bars, animal crackers, dry cereal, cans of tuna and/or pudding.
- can opener
- Swiss Army Knife or a serrated knife in a protected covering (you can make one out of cardboard)

For the **Paper Products Bag** (buy recycled products, if possible)—

- cereal—a kind that most of you will eat and an assortment of single serving boxes for variety
- paper plates, bowls, cups (not styrafoam)
- paper towels, napkins (optional, as you can use the paper towels)
- assorted plastic silverware
- empty bread bags & other reusable bags

Food Tips:

* **Be sure to save bread & other bags, crackers, catsup, mustard, & other small packets that you receive in restaurants but aren't able to use (you'll be surprised how much of this stuff you'll accumulate and how handy it may come in later).**
* **It's better to replace items than to buy large sizes—especially perishables**
* **Grocery stores & markets may be hard to find and get to in large cities, so if possible stop in a smaller town before you get there to get basic items or at a gas station with attached shop—you can get your tank filled at the same time, so you won't have to worry about that!**

V. OPTIONAL ITEMS
When In Doubt, Leave it out!

These are the items you might have an occasion to wish you hadn't left at home—be careful on this one!

Optional Items List:

- sports equipment—fishing gear, tennis rackets, golf clubs, etc.
- stamps—will save you hunting for a post office or paying extra, when you want to send post cards
- alarm clock—at most places you can simply leave a wake-up call
- beach toys
- potty item—whatever you come up with, make sure it doesn't leak (a large coffee can, double bagged with Zip Locks or other plastic bags, secured with it's own lid, works well)
- baby equipment—that will be a list in itself, you're on your own if you decide to take Baby!

  Don't forget the car seats.

VI. THE LAST MINUTE BEFORE YOU LEAVE HOME LIST "Did We Unplug The Hairdryer?"

- Give itinerary to a relative
- Also give itinerary (and a key if you like) to a reliable neighbor and have them pick up any advertisements stuck in your door. In winter have them park in your driveway or make tire marks when it snows.
- Stop mail & newspapers or make arrangements for someone to pick up
- Make arrangements for any pets
- Set some lights on timers
- Water plants—make arrangements if they'll need watering while you are away
- Unplug appliances

****Special Notes of Caution—Think Small**

"Bigger is not necessarily Better" holds true for other items besides food. Remember you'll be living with and carrying this stuff!

Once you have perfected all these lists, be sure to hang on to them—it will save you lots of time on your next trip! And remember, if you should forget something, no need to panic, there really isn't anything you can't buy along the way except maybe the addresses of your friends back home (for postcards), and you can probably call someone for those!

CHAPTER 3

ORGANIZING, CAR, WAGON, OR VAN (Learning to Love It!)

Organization is the key to surviving in your mini home whether it be a small car or roomy van. Since you already know what you need to take, the idea now is to have it where you'll need it, when you need it! Here, vans and station wagons have an advantage, as your storage area is accessible without stopping. Cars, on the other hand, will occasionally need an additional stop to get something from the trunk, but if possible you should try and have the things you're likely to need on a regular basis (such as water, snacks, and sweaters) in the passenger area.

HOW TO PACK—Who's Baggage Is It?

Inside Your Home On Wheels—

This is where you will want to pack your most frequently used items, including; your Main Survival Items, some General Items, and some Personal Items (see below and Ch. 2 for more information). Your Main Survival items should be stored as compactly as possible near the navigator, otherwise known as the non-driving parent; he or she gets to be in charge of disbursing such items. If you have a divided front seat, you can store some things in between, where they are conveniently out of the way. If you have a small car you will no doubt have to use some of them for foot rests. In our minivan we were able to keep our small cooler and food box (Girl Scout cookie box with handle was perfect) in between the front seats; the top of the cooler could be used as a table surface, and current travel maps, info, and lists (stored in folders, envelopes, or small flat bags) were tucked around it. If you have a station wagon or small van, you may be able to store some of these things just behind the back seat, as long as a responsible member of your party is able to reach them. The water jug needs to be near your designated "water boy"; this can be a responsible older child. But you may want to keep an eye on the number of hand-outs—remember the idea is to eliminate frequent stops!

Main Survival Items—

- cooler
- food & snack box
- paper products bag
- water jug
- maps & information
- purse

Frequently Used General Items like the lap tray, camera, tape recorder, sun screen, bug spray, and other travel information can go under the seats or in any accessible niche you can find. If you have to resort to your trunk for carrying a few of these items, make your choices carefully.

Frequently Used General Items—

- lap tray
- camera
- tape recorder
- Goody Bag
- first aid kit
- flashlight
- sun screen
- bug spray
- additional travel information

Personal Items, including pillow and Things To Do Bag need to be stored in one's own sitting area. This works best if kids generally sit in the same place, so if possible get your kids to go along with this plan. If they need to keep switching in order "to be fair", it will be more bothersome. Drink cups need to go by each person's seat; if your car doesn't have holders for them, purchase the inexpensive plastic ones that hang on the window ledges. Hats can go on your back shelf or on top of the general heap if you have a van or wagon; sweaters or sweatshirts also need to be handy in cooler weather.

Frequently Used Personal Items –
- pillow (kids)
- Things To Do Bag (kids)
- hats (for the sun)
- sweaters or sweatshirts
- drink cups

For The Trunk –

As mentioned in Chapter 2, Seldom Used General Items (coats, rain gear, laundry stuff, extra shoes, towels, etc.) can be grouped, stuffed into bags, and stashed in the back of the trunk, along with any Optional Items you wish to take. Hopefully you will still have room to throw in the Seldom Used (during the day) Personal Items such as suitcases, and kids' sleeping bags if you need them. If your cooler & paper products bag did not fit in the car, either squeeze them into the trunk, invest in smaller ones, or leave some of the Optional Items at home!

Seldom Used General Items—in trunk
- coats
- raingear & umbrella
- tablecloth
- laundry & dishwashing soap
- extra shoes
- towels & any beach toys
- winter emergency gear (seasonal)

Seldom Used Personal Items—for motel
- suitcases and/or clothing duffel bags
- sleeping bags (kids)
- tote bag
- assorted beauty products & accessories (in a sturdy bag)
- laundry bag

Optional Items—(take as few as possible)
- sports equipment—fishing gear, etc.
- alarm clock
- beach toys

UNLOADING – "Where's the Pool?"

Now that we have the car organized, loading and unloading should be a snap, even if your hotel/motel room is located 7 floors up and through a maze of corridors! However, if you get lucky and get a room with a parking spot outside your door, it is definitely cause to celebrate; just don't forget the following basic guidelines. The idea is to be able to unload in one trip – you will be amazed at the smoothness of the system! The plan goes like this:

Arrive at motel and check in – kids will want to check out the facilities at this time; try to limit them to the lobby area or leave in car with an adult.

Proceed to designated parking area.

Unload – each person carrying own bag(s) needed in motel and one other item if possible (cooler, paper products bag, and water jug if it needs to be refilled). Most items forgotten at this time and information to plan the next day's activities can be brought in later when returning from dinner or shopping.

Send reliable older kid(s) for ice to refill container.

Explore new home.

Plan dinner and evening activities.

Swim, Enjoy!

Dinner and/or Shopping Run

Go over plan for next day, get weather forecast. Plan clothing if possible and update expense book. Call office to leave wake-up call for 1 hour prior to desired time of departure.

LOADING – Beat the Clock!

The morning plan is a little trickier, as time is of the essence. But you will be congratulating yourselves when this plan all comes together and you can actually get going in less than an hour (from the time you get up until you're on the road, and that includes a nutritious breakfast)! Of course that's figuring your crew is old enough to be somewhat self sufficient!

The key to success with the Morning Plan all centers around the bathroom schedule – production must keep moving! Showers and hair washing should be taken care of the night before and only the basic necessities allowed – hat's off to the designers who separate the sink and mirror area from the shower and toilet; that alone can save precious time in a hectic morning schedule. Teenagers who require a lengthy beauty routine before they can be seen in public should be provided with some sort of car mirror. The morning plan should go something like this:

Parents get up—one starts the bathroom routine, the other lays out the breakfast things (see ON THE MOVE in Ch. 4 for alternate super-fast breakfast idea).

Bathroom parent starts kids on bathroom routine, goes to office to check out, picks up free coffee if available.

Everyone juggles dressing, eating, and packing with bathroom time—keeping it occupied until everyone has had a turn; all packed items should be placed near the door.

Send available older kid for ice; fill container—also water jug if necessary.

Everyone check around for forgotten items—especially drawers, under beds, and bathroom area (wet swim suits!). Be sure to throw in any freebies—such as notepaper, soap, shampoo, and plastic water glasses (leave the ashtrays, towels, etc.!)

Leave key on dresser.

Everyone grab own bags and at least one other—you're on your way!

If you have loaded and unloaded in one trip, congratulate yourselves—you've mastered the system. If not, keep working to improve your efficiency and time. With such common goals, you'll find members of your party will work together better with more of a cooperative spirit instead of being afraid they might be doing more work than someone else.

CHAPTER 4
EN ROUTE
"Are We There Yet?"

Since the Luxury Travel Plan for the Unrich and Unfamous is based on **value** (getting the most vacation time for the $), once you're on the road the only acceptable reasons for stopping are the following: tourist attractions & scenery (can include just enjoying a special moment), food essentials, if a kid is sick or needs help, car trouble, switching drivers, and of course, emergencies. Exercise, rest stops, and getting things from your trunk should be included in the previously mentioned stops. The less time spent "getting there", the more time you'll have to spend at your final stop of the day, hopefully a place that you have selected with your family's enjoyment in mind.

WHERE TO STAY
Variety is the spice of life

MOTELS & HOTELS

Although it's nice to know what to expect, motel chains can also be boring if you stay in the same kind every night. Sometimes it's good to stick with something predictable, and there are enough chains so that you can still have some variety in your itinerary. BUT if you really want your trip to be interesting, be sure to include some unusual local resorts or hotels. The rating systems in books and travel clubs we have found to be quite reliable and often these places are comparable in cost to the chains, but are more fun to explore and have different kinds of activities available. We have found tennis courts, Par 3 Golf, horseback riding, and covered bridges over picturesque rocky streams at "non-chain" motels. Things you need to consider when making your choices: close proximity to your route, public transportation accessibility if desired, your budget (obviously, the less you spend here the more $ for meals and fun stuff), how much time your family will be spending there, and what is available close by or at the motel itself for your family to do. Many motels are now offering special programs for kids, as well as babysitting services.

For example: If you've had a day of mainly driving, you will want a place that offers interesting things to do; however, if you've had a busy day of sightseeing and other activities, you may only need the basics—it would be a waste to spend more for a place featuring extras. Also, if the weather is likely to be cold or miserable, look for something with indoor activities available, etc.

Sleeping arrangements can be handled in various ways depending on the number, gender, and ages of your children. Your most economical rooms for families will have 2 double beds with cots available. If your kids do not handle sleeping together very well, try letting them take turns having the big bed all to themselves (they love it!), and the other nights they will be content to find a spot on the floor for their sleeping bag.

Motel Tips:

* **Never use drawers—takes more time & too easy to forget to check when leaving**
* **Always leave key in same place—our "key place" is on the TV**
* **Be on the lookout for extra charges, as for local telephone calls and/or some TV channels**
* **Take advantage of all the freebies (coffee, continental breakfasts, etc.)**
* **Have kids locate fire escapes**

FRIENDS & RELATIVES

It can be tempting to want to stay with friends and relatives in the areas you are visiting, as they always seem to want to have you, and you will save $. **But—a word of caution**—if your time is limited, it may be best to rent your own place and get together for an activity or visit. This way you are more free to decide what **you** want to do. When you stay with friends, they may feel responsible for planning your itinerary and showing you a good time—and it might not be what **you** had in mind at all.

OTHER OPTIONS

Other options for inexpensive and interesting places to stay include: Youth Hostels, Elder Hostels, college campuses (some rent out dorm rooms), fraternity & sorority houses (if you belong), YMCAs, Lighthouses, and Bed & Breakfasts (although not always inexpensive); however, some of these seem to work out better for the single or couples travelers. For families, you might want to look into the new KOA cabins, condos that people are willing to rent, or home exchange clubs. For information, the phone numbers listed at the end of Chapter 6 will be helpful. Good options of travel opportunities for young people continue to be Work/Study or Travel/Study Programs and Exchange Programs.

$ SAVING TIPS ON LODGING—watch for & ask about

* **Off season rates**
* **Kids and/or teens sleep free**
* **Free meals or discounts**
* **Special room rates: weekend specials, super saver, corporate rates, at Holiday Inn: Priority Club & Great Rates, etc.**
* **Discounts & coupons through a travel club such as AAA, the AARP organization, or guidebooks & magazines**
* **Special programs for kids**

Safety Tip!

* **Don't wander about cities alone—be especially careful about where you go at night, try to stay where there are a lot of people.**

WHERE TO EAT
"Mom, I'm still hungry!"

DINING OUT

Since you only have one opportunity a day for this (see Introduction), it's important to make good choices—as with motels, keep variety in mind. First you will need to decide what meal it will be. Generally it will be dinner, unless you have an all day excursion when carrying along the makings for lunch would really not be very convenient. You will want to take advantage of the Best Meal Deals (and surprisingly it isn't always fast food), so that you can occasionally splurge on local specialities (When in Rome. . .). After all, you've come this far so don't skimp when it comes to important things—try the buffalo burgers at Wall Drug, the seafood at Fisherman's Wharf, and the gumbo in New Orleans. Remember, this is a luxury vacation!

Ask at your motel for recommendations—they can often tell you the places where local people go—usually the best food for the money. Sometimes they will have coupons or special deals for children in their own restaurant. Better yet, ask local people like store clerks who have no vested interest in your motel. If your children don't eat much, look for places with children's menus, check the phone book and call if necessary. If they are older and tend to always be starving, look for all-you-can-eat buffet meals. Many places have wonderful Sunday Brunches, and a snack may be all you'll need later in the day! Other places where you are likely to find good food at reasonable prices are ethnic areas, malls for variety, or places near college campuses. As for your local coupons, they probably won't apply—so you might as well leave them at home.

Eating Tips:

* **Many restaurants now post their menus outside; take the time to look them over before going inside.**
* **Those with small appetites can divide a meal.**

* **If you are able to eat your big meal at noon—it will cost less.**

ORDERING IN

Room service can be tempting, and even though this is a luxury trip and you are entitled to splurge now and then, do you really need it? After all, your family has been trained to handle your own room service quite well, and they might rather enjoy a special treat at the Ice Cream Parlor some afternoon or evening.

The following nutritious ideas work well for in-room dining:

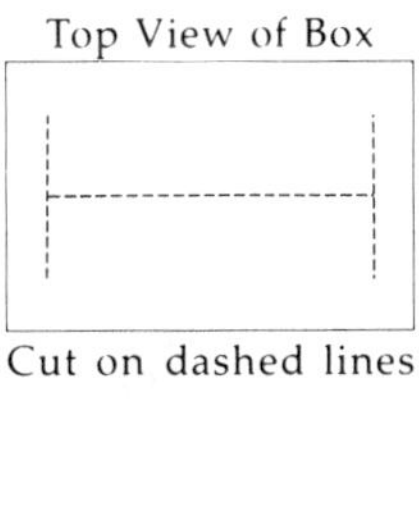

Breakfast—juice, cereal, milk for cereal—individual serving boxes of cereal can be opened carefully with your serrated knife as shown in diagram (saves bowls, but have napkin handy as they occasionally leak)

Dinner—easy, and one of our tried & true family favorites: buy container of macaroni salad, add can of tuna or chicken & cut up tomato (mix in a container or on individual plates); serve with bread, milk, & canned pudding for dessert.

Other ideas: buy a few veggies & make a chef salad (check your supplies of cheese & lunch meat or use canned chicken). Cut up some canned peaches and add to a store bought chicken salad. Or, mix your own fruit salad—have each person select a different piece of fruit to be chopped up, and serve with a sandwich or purchased fried chicken. There's always canned fruit; try adding a small can of crushed pineapple to some cottage cheese. It's always nice to buy some special bread to compliment your salad dinners, or select a cheese spread & crackers. If you plan on doing this sort of meal very often, you may wish to bring along a plastic bowl for your mixing.

Have a deli supper (choose an assortment of items from the grocery store deli) or make special sandwiches by using pita bread or sub buns and some interesting fillers. Naturally, you can always resort to pizza.

For dessert try adding some cut up peaches to vanilla pudding or pick out something special in the bakery department. If you need a **snack idea**, most kids enjoy popcorn or salsa with tortilla chips.

Occasionally a motel will have a microwave available, which will open up lots of possibilities, or if you really want to be ambitious, you can bring a small one along.

Be creative—you never know what great ideas you may get just walking through the grocery store!

ON THE MOVE—Picnics & In-Car Meals

Breakfast—If you're especially anxious to get an early start or if your family is tired of the usual cereal menu, give them juice in your room; then enjoy bananas and bagels or bread & peanut butter in the car.

Lunches—Get the lap tray out and go into sandwich production—you can be fairly accommodating here, as you generally have lots of time. Try to change your sandwich selections and fruit from time to time, and of course, always have peanut butter & jelly available as a standby. If you want your kids to have something other than water to drink, this can be done when the car is stopped for other reasons.

Sometimes it's nice to picnic when you're on a day excursion. Select light weight lunch items to carry in your shoulder **tote bag.** Drinks are heavy so either buy them as you go or carry paper cups and find drinking fountains en route (remember it's important to drink a lot of water on hot days). If no tables will be available, carry your table cloth to spread out in a shady spot on the ground. This saves both time and money and worked especially well for us on the Mall in Washington, D.C.

> * **Tip—When using your tote bag you don't need to carry your purse—simply transfer the items you will need and leave it behind in a safe place, like the trunk of your car.**

FOOD SHOPPING
(Getting to know the local grocery)

The best time for this is after dinner out, or if dining in, find a local grocery or Quick Stop for needed dinner items and to replenish the **food box** and **cooler**. Most grocery stores now have a deli section that usually has an interesting variety of things for lunch or dinner. If the store doesn't have one, do the best you can in the dairy cases. Buy only supplies needed for a few days, especially perishables. When the Quick Stop is part of a gas station, you can really save time if one person takes care of filling the gas tank while someone else does the shopping.

$ SAVING TIPS ON FOOD -

- **Soft drinks—If not eating in the restaurant, you can buy the largest size available and use your own paper cups to divide it up.**
- **Things To Save—empty bread bags and, if not used— napkins, crackers, condiment packets, etc. They might come in handy later.**

ON THE ROAD—Again!

ON-GOING ACTIVITIES
Reading, Writing, & 'rithmetic

Reading—Visit your local library before you leave so that all family members have an adequate supply of books. Young children should have books they can enjoy on their own, and an on-going story book that older family members can read to them. Pamphlets and information you pick up on the way about the places you are visiting, also make good in-car reading material.

Writing—Everyone should be involved in keeping a **Log** of the trip. Young children should have their own notebook to write or draw about what they see on a daily basis (a page a day)—a folder that also has pockets works well and gives them a place to keep special pamphlets they pick up. Have some special stickers in your **Goody Bag**—give them one for their log every time you go 100 miles, to put on the appropriate page. Older family members can keep one notebook and take turns making the entries on a daily basis. You will enjoy reading it when you get home, reliving the daily highlights and even the difficult times.

Other writing activities include postcards or notes to friends, drawing or coloring, doing activity books, etc. One adult should be keeping **daily records of expenses** (food, gas, lodging, entertainment, etc.) so that you're keeping as close to your budget goal as possible.

'rithmetic—on-going car games such as how many different license plates you can see, counting the number of McDonalds or Wall Drug signs, or practically anything you choose—like even practicing your times tables!

* **Tip—If you have a van and have a hard time communicating with those in the very back, we found an inexpensive walkie talkie telephone to be fun!**

SPECIAL EVENTS—"Mom, I'm Bored!"

When the usual activities don't seem to be working, before resorting to the **Goody Bag**, try one or more of the following ideas for a change of pace:

Car games—many of these games can be played by the group as a whole, such as the ABC Sign Game, looking for different state license plates, types of sports cars, or different styles of roofs. If you want a little competition, try having teams, or dividing up by having individuals look for things only on their own side of the road, or with games involving written lists, just arrange them in a different order for each player. To get you started, there are 50 favorite car games explained at the end of this chapter. Modify any of them to best suit your family's needs or try making up your own!

Sing Alongs—a little camp booklet or papers with words of songs that you've collected can come in handy. Song themes can be fun, such as: on rainy days sing songs you know about rain, out west sing cowboy songs, sing appropriate songs for cities and states you may be passing through like " O k l a h o m a" or "I Left My Heart in San Francisco". You can also have a good time starting a new song with a word from the one currently being sung, playing Name That Tune, or singing favorites like "Old McDonald" or "99 Bottles of Pop on the Wall", or just trying to remember as many nursery rhymes as you can.

The Tape Recorder—you can enjoy a variety of tapes, such as: story tapes for children, fun tapes like Bill Cosby or Bob Newhart (visit your library), and interesting tapes you've made with relatives. Even more fun will be making your own tape. Interview family members about what they remember or favorite places on the trip, or do pretend interviews of interesting people you have encountered or famous people.

> * **Tip—Many of the games in this chapter will also work well while waiting in restaurants or long lines.**

SOUVENIRS—"What? No GIFT Shop?"

This book would be lacking, if it didn't mention (the dreaded word) **SOUVENIRS**, as you and your children will be bombarded with shops full of expensive trinkets at every turn—often the same item can be found from Maine to California with the local name stamped on, but the always familiar Made in Japan, Taiwan, etc.

Although it is impossible to steer clear of all these places, nor should you (it's part of our culture), you can set limits—which ones?, how much time?, etc. Assuming some purchasing will be allowed, some lessons that can be taught here are: setting priorities, making choices, and value (quality of item for the $). You will have to decide what's best for your family, but what I suggest (it works for us) is setting a limit and letting each child select something special to help him remember the trip. They may use much of the trip getting ideas, making a final choice towards the end, or they might find something right away. Anything else that they " just have to have" they would need to use their own money.

Keep in mind that some of the interesting things you might want to collect are either inexpensive or free, such as: stones, match books, decals, or pennants. Whatever you should decide, kids should understand that visiting souvenir shops is **not** the main purpose of your trip!

BE FLEXIBLE—Smell the Roses

As much as planning ahead is important, don't be completely inflexible as you are bound to hear about other wonderful happenings along the way, and there are always unscheduled events to keep your trip interesting. So be sure to take the time to stop and smell the roses, even if it means making some changes in your itinerary (Remember, you have allowed for this). Your unplanned experiences may be some of your most memorable!

Let me tell you about one of our experiences. We were staying at a resort motel near the Grand Canyon when we met Claude and Laird on the tennis courts, one of whom was an archaeologist. They convinced us that our planned route from there through the Grand Canyon and then on to Mesa Verde, which included some backtracking, could be changed to a more direct route which also included Monument Valley, real dinosaur tracks (you have to believe an archaeologist), the Four Corners, and a stay at a Holiday Inn on an

Indian Reservation where not far away we observed horses grazing on the lawn at the local Burger King. We only changed one reservation, but it added so much to our trip! Local people can really be helpful. Talk to them; you'll be amazed at what you will learn. "Thanks", Claude and Laird wherever you are!

50 NIFTY CAR GAMES FOR TRAVELERS

A Game List may seem silly, but when traveling a sense of humor is a must! These games are listed by categories with the easiest ones presented first – the further down in each category, the more appropriate for older kids. As you will see, some are similar. Try variations or make up your own games – whatever is fun for your family!

NUMBER GAMES

Find The Most – The idea is to see who can count the most of something within a specified time limit. Players choose different objects to count, such as: red cars vs blue cars, cows vs horses, trucks vs vans, etc. Older kids might enjoy Chevrolets vs Fords or license plates of one state vs another.

Find The Numbers 1 – ? on Signs, Billboards, etc.

Odd or Even—Players put their hands behind their backs and count "1-2-3-go". On "go" they all hold out their hands with any number of fingers extended. Adding up all the extended fingers, they decide if the number is odd or even. No one wins or loses.

Number Facts—Practice reciting math tables—addition or multiplication, at whatever level is appropriate for your children.

Math Mind-Joggers—make up story problems; find some advanced brainteasers for older kids.

GUESSING GAMES

I Spy—Someone starts by saying I see something _____ (filling in the blank with a clue such as a color). The others try to guess the object. Whoever guesses correctly starts the next round. * **Note**—if car is moving, choose objects inside the car, as what you see outside won't be there for long!

ABC Sign Game—Starting at the beginning of the alphabet, look for each letter on roadsigns. Individuals shout them out as they see each one, and either jot them down or start with the whole alphabet and cross them off as they see them. The idea is to see who can spot all the letters first; you can eliminate difficult letters like "Q" and "Z" if you like.

Twenty Questions–Someone selects a subject and gives one clue as to whether it is animal, vegetable, or mineral. The others have 20 questions with which to guess the subject. The questions can only be answered yes or no.

Family Trivia–Someone asks a question relating to the family–could be about pets, friends, vacations, or a really good idea would be questions concerning relatives you may be visiting on your trip (What's the name of their cat?, etc.) Whoever guesses correctly is next.

Car Identification Game–See how many cars you can identify.

What am I? Someone picks a category such as food, vehicles, something found in nature, etc.; then gives two clues. "I am a useful object; I have four legs and a head. What am I?" (a bed) Everyone gets two guesses. If players are stumped, give another clue. Whoever guesses correctly goes next; if players are still stumped, the current player gets another turn.

Who Am I? Same as *What am I,* only give clues for and try to guess a famous person.

Highway Signs–How many different ones can you find in a specific time? Draw a sketch. Later discuss what they mean. Look for the new international signs, which use symbols rather than words.

Roof Game—How many styles of roofs can you find? Draw a sketch of each. Examples: barn style, gables, dormers, etc.

MEMORY GAMES

I'm Going On A Trip—Someone starts by saying, "I'm going on a trip or I'm going to (name a specific place) and I'm going to take a _____." (Fill in the blank with a specific item like a suitcase.) The next player repeats that sentence and adds another item to the list, such as a toothbrush. A player is out of the game when he forgets an item or confuses the order.

Spelling Bee—Adults think up words for kids to spell—at their particular level.

Ghost—First player has a word in mind, such as "store"; he says the first letter "s". Each player adds a letter with his own word in mind (Example—second player might say "l" with the word "sleep" in mind), trying to avoid completing a word. Whoever ends up completing a word gets a letter from the word GHOST, starting with a "G". Whenever someone has received all the letters from the word G-H-O-S-T, he loses or is out of the game.

States & Capitals—Try to list all of the states east or west of the Mississippi River. Then try to name the capitals.

WORD GAMES

Sausages—One person is "it". The others take turns asking him all kinds of questions, but he must always answer with the word "sausages". If he laughs (or if you want to make it really difficult, if he even smiles), another player becomes "it".

Gossip—Whisper a sentence to the next person, that person repeats it to the next, and so on. The last person says what he heard out loud.

Geography—Someone says the name of a place (city, state, country, river, park, etc.). Next player names a place that begins with the last letter of the previous player's word (Example: "Rocky Mountains—San Francisco—Oklahoma"). If a player repeats someone else's word they are out.

Alphabet Soup—Someone starts by saying a word that begins with "A". Continue going around the car naming words that start with the same letter until a player is stumped. That player then starts the next letter of the alphabet. How far can your family go?

Rhyme Time—First player chooses a simple word like "lake". The others think of as many words as they can that rhyme with it. Then the following player thinks of a new word for making the next rhyme.

Opposites—First player gives a word like "on"; next player says the opposite "off". Players work in teams to see how many opposites they can get.

Brainstorming—Someone says a word like "cold". Other players say the first thing that pops into their minds, such as "winter, ice cream, refrigerator, etc."

PENCIL & PAPER

Tic Tac Toe—classic game for two. If your kids don't know it already, teach them how to play.

Treasure Hunt—Someone makes up a word list of 10 things that might be seen from the car. Each person gets the same list, but in a different order and must find the items chronologically as they appear on his list. Whoever gets through his/her list first is the winner. For variety, try a particular category such as car items (Examples: a car like yours, one with the hood open, one making a left hand turn, etc.), or nature things, etc. for the list.

Lengthy List—Same as *Treasure Hunt*, but everyone has the same order on their list. This time, the first person to see something gets to cross it off his list and the others must find another one in order to count it.

Make Something Out Of This—Someone draws a number, letter, or scribble and gives it to someone else, who then tries to make it into a silly picture.

Dots—(works best with 2 people) someone makes several equal rows of dots on a piece of paper about 1/4 inch apart. Players take turns drawing 1 line between any 2 dots, either horizontally or vertically, attempting to potentially form complete squares. When a player's line completes a square, he puts his initial in the square and gets another turn. When all the squares are completed, the player who has initialed the most squares is the winner. (This game can be made any size—I recommend starting with 16–20 dots.)

Hangman—Someone thinks of a word and draws on a piece of paper the correct amount of blanks for each letter. Other players take turns trying to guess the letters and eventually, the word. A simple stick gallows is drawn, and for each wrong letter that a player guesses, he draws a part of a body on the gallows. The drawing starts with a circle for the head, followed by a line for the body, then lines for each arm and leg (If more than six guesses are desired add more body parts, like feet or a hat). If the body is completed before the word is guessed, that player gets to try another word.

Word Hunt—Players select a long word like hamburger, mountain, etc. Everyone writes it on the top of his page and using only the letters that are in that word, makes up as many other words as he/she can.

Alphabet Marathon—Each player writes all the letters in the alphabet in a column. When all have finished, they begin to write a word for each letter. The first one done is the winner and gets to read his list.

MUSIC & ACTING
tape some of this for fun!

Rhythm

Clapping Game—Take turns clapping a rhythm and have others try to copy it.

Rock, Scissors, Paper—Two players hold one hand behind their backs and say "rock, scissors, paper" in unison. As soon as they say the last syllable, they, at the same time, quickly thrust their hands out front in a certain way to represent either rock (a fist), scissors (middle & index finger form a (V), or paper (flat hand with palm down). The idea is to see who beats whom: paper covers rock, rock breaks scissors, & scissors cut paper. You can do this over & over just for fun or you can keep score.

Categories—Players set up a rhythm by slapping their thighs twice, clapping twice, and snapping their fingers twice (once with each hand), in that order. The first player starts by saying "Categories" when they snap fingers; on the next finger snaps he says "Names Of". And the next time he gives the name of a category like fruits, colors, states, etc. Going around in order each player must name something that fits the category. If a player misses naming something on the snaps, he is out and the next player starts a new category, until all but one player are eliminated.

IMAGINATION

Finish the Story—Someone starts telling a story, trying to be as creative as possible and stops at a crucial point. The next player continues with his own creative version, and stops. This goes on until you have a long, imaginative story and a player decides to end it. You might want to tape this and play it back for fun.

Sky Shapes—Look at the clouds; share what you think some of them look like.

Make Believe—Someone asks an imaginative question and the others give their answers. Examples: If you could be an animal, what would you be & why?, If you could make three wishes, what would they be? If you saw a Martian, what would you say? If your car could talk, what would it say? etc.

The House Game—Pick out an interesting house along the way. Make up a story about who lives there, what they might be doing & why, etc.

What A Guy—Tell each person in the car something you like about him. (A good time for this one is when passengers are starting to get on each other's nerves.)

Silence—Try not to talk; first one to break the silence loses and ends the game.

Commercials—Make up commercials for places you've been. Tape for fun.

SING-A-LONG

Sing Every Song You Know—The name says it all.

Name That Tune—Take turns humming a tune and have the others guess what it is.

Sing in Rounds—*Row, Row, Row Your Boat,* and any others you can think of.

CARD GAMES

War—(works best for 2 players)—all the cards in the deck are dealt out and each player puts his cards in a stack face down in front of him. On each turn they simultaneously turn over the top card and the player with the highest card takes the others & adds them to the bottom of his pile. If they turn up the same card, it's "war", and the players with matching cards place the next 3 cards from their pile face down on the warring card & the next card, face up. High card takes the lot. If by chance they match cards again, they do another war and the winner collects all the cards from both wars. The game ends when a player has all the cards, or if you decide to quit sooner, the player with the most cards is the winner.

Go Fish – All players are dealt 7 cards; the rest are placed in a pile face down (fish pile). The player to the left of the dealer begins by asking any player if he has a particular card that matches one in his hand. Example: "Do you have any fives?" If the questioned player has the requested card he must give it to the questioner, who then makes the pair and sets it aside to be counted later. He continues to ask for cards until the person asked does not have the requested card, who then says "Go Fish". The first player picks up any card from the fish pile, and adds it to his hand unless it is the requested card, in which case he makes the pair and continues his turn. Otherwise, play continues with the next player to the left asking for cards. When all the cards have been paired, the player with the most pairs is the winner.

Old Maid – This game can be played with a regular deck of cards. Choose a card like a queen to be the old maid; then remove the other three queens. The rest of the cards are dealt out to the players. Players match up all their pairs and set them aside; then, starting with the dealer, they take turns going around holding up their cards so the player on their left can't see them and have that person draw a card. If the card matches one that he has in his hand, he sets the pair aside; otherwise it remains in his hand. Play continues until all the cards have been paired & discarded except the old maid. Whoever ends up with her, loses.

Crazy Eights—Dealer gives out 8 cards face down to each player; he places the remaining cards face down in a stack, turning the top one over to make a discard pile. The person to the left of the dealer goes first by selecting from his hand, a card that is either the same number or suit of the upturned card, and places it on top of it. If he has no card that plays, he may play an "8" and call out any suit he wishes to make it. If he has no "8", he must draw a card and add it to his hand unless it plays on the discard pile. Play continues with the person on his left. The winner is the first to discard all his cards. (If the face-down pile is used up, reshuffle the discard pile & turn it over.)

CHAPTER 5

WHERE IT'S AT in the U.S. and Canada

We are indeed fortunate to live in a country that has such a variety and wealth of awesome natural wonders. Add to that the amazing creations that men have built over the years—historical displays, scientific achievements, and attractions just for fun. Not only do we live in this wondrous place, but we are free to come and go as we please, with most of these exciting places available to us at our convenience—it's incredible!

It would be impossible to include in this book all the worthwhile places to visit, so just because something does not appear on this list doesn't mean it isn't a MUST SEE item, as one is never able to see everything he or she might like – due to time and other factors. But what does appear in this list are the places we or close family members were able to visit and are willing to recommend. I encourage you to add to this list as you venture out on your own travels and pass along any great findings to others. Also, don't forget to take time for the little adventures that aren't listed in the travel books, such as having a mid-summer snowball fight or sliding down a roadside snow patch in the Rockies, looking for sportscars in Beverly Hills, checking out plush hotel lobbies in Toronto, watching waves crashing on rocks on the Oregon Coast, or hunting for a famous picture such as the row houses in San Francisco. Not only is the price right, but these outings may prove to be some of your most memorable experiences.

> Some of the many unique and/or impressive hotel lobbies which you might want to visit if you happen to be in the neighborhood are: The Four Seasons & the Beverly Hills Hotel in Tinseltown, the victorian style Hotel Jerome in Aspen, CO (onetime silvertown, now famous as a resort – especially skiing – 800/525-2052), the Fairmont on Nob Hill (TV Show – *Hotel*) in San Francisco, the Royal York in Toronto, or the Peabody in Memphis

(famous for it's daily marching of ducks to the lobby fountain)!

MUST SEES

Disney World & Epcot Center (FL)—the Disney experience is a must, always fun and interesting for the whole family. (407/824-4321) You can even combine this with a **Caribbean Cruise*** (1-800-888-6759). If you don't plan to get to California, you will want to include **Universal Studios.**

Grand Canyon (AZ)—the dramatic vastness of the area is impressive. To best appreciate it, take advantage of various trips to the bottom, white water rafting, or a helicopter ride. (Reservations for these special outings are necessary many months ahead.)

Mackinac Island (MI)—the closest thing in this country to going back in time, as no cars are allowed on the island. The historic landmark, the Grand Hotel, with it's famous porch, dominates the island as you approach via ferry or hydroplane. We enjoy renting bikes for a ride around the island; carriage rides are fun too—and less strenuous on a hot July day! Be sure to visit the fort and sample the famous fudge. (For a free travel planner of the Mackinac/Straits area call 800-666-0160)

* **Note—Side trips referred to under various points of interest (italicized) are indicated by Bold Type**

Niagara Falls (NY & CAN)—truly one of the great wonders of the world—best view from the Canadian side. Try to view it at night with the colored lights focused on it as well as during the daytime. Ride the "Maid of the Mist" to really appreciate its magnitude!

Washington, D.C.—lots to see here and most of it's free! Here your family can enjoy a United States History lesson practically anywhere you go. A good example is being able to view the original *Declaration of Independence* and *U.S. Constitution* at the National Archives Building. In the city, there are special tours of the White House, the Capitol, and the F.B.I. Headquarters (Your senator or congressman will be happy to get you passes for these if you request them in advance—as early as possible. If that doesn't work out, try your hotel concierge). On your visit be sure to include the Library of Congress, Supreme Court Building, Bureau of Engraving & Printing, and several of the Smithsonian Institute's (202/357-2020) many museums—especially the National Air and Space Museum (the world's finest collection of flying machines & aircraft, including the Wright Brothers' 1903 Flyer & Apollo II 202/357-2700), Museum of American History, and the Natural History Museum.

At the other end of The Mall you will want to see the Washington Monument (although you may have a long wait if you decide to ride to the top), and the Lincoln Memorial & Viet Nam Wall, both very touching emotionally. Also if you like, take in one of the many free concerts around town; during the summer

Army, Navy, Air Force, & Marine Bands perform at 8:00 pm nightly at the Washington Monument and by the west steps of the Capitol. All of these places are within walking distance and not too difficult if you plan to cover a different area each day; however, public transportation is available. Driving is not recommended—the Metro Subway system is great! Many motels & hotels are located close to Metro stations—much priceless time can be wasted driving, getting lost, and searching for a rare parking space.

As a side trip you will want to visit **Mt. Vernon**, George Washington's notable plantation on the Potomac and **Arlington National Cemetery** with the Tomb of the Unknown Soldier, J.F. Kennedy's grave, and the memorial dedicated to the astronauts—another emotional experience. If you have enough time and haven't seen any Giant Pandas, try to get to the **National Zoo** (202/357-2020) during feeding time.

Yellowstone National Park (WY/MT)—you're not likely to see bears as in the past; but other interesting wildlife, the beauty of the Canyon & Falls, and the variety of hot pools & geysers will amaze you. Be sure to go inside the rustic Old Faithful Lodge—they just don't build them like that anymore!

ADD-ONS—in your travels, you may find something that you feel belongs in this section. Feel free to write about it here:

DEFINITELY WORTHWHILE

NORTHEAST

Acadia National Park at Bar Harbor (ME)—an unusual combination of awesome cliffs and surf pounding against them—whale watching excursions available from the Golden Anchor Inn Pier (207/288-9794).

Annapolis (MD)—located on Chesapeake Bay, the downtown area is charming, with specialty shops around the city dock area; Windjammer Cruises available, with or without overnight accommodations. Tour the naval academy—don't miss the beautiful chapel and the crypt of John Paul Jones located below.

Baltimore (MD)—the revitalized Inner Harbor offers the wonderful National Aquarium, Maryland Science Center, shopping pavilions, ethnic eateries, old boats to explore, boat rides available (including one to Fort McHenry, where Francis Scott Key wrote the "Star Spangled Banner"), and you can take a water taxi!

Belfast (ME)— victorian homes & culture—artists, craftsmen, writers—check out the Opera House & summer festival.

Boston (MA) – history will come alive as you take the Historic Walking Tour through the city visiting places like the Granary Burying Ground, Paul Revere's house, and the Old North Church; and continuing across the bridge you will have the opportunity to explore the beautifully maintained ship, The U.S.S. Constitution. At the Boston Museum of Science you can build a skeleton with real bones, meet a live Boa Constricter, and watch spectacular lightning shows (617/523–6664). Another interesting area is the Beacon Hill District. Driving in this town is difficult, so leave your car at your motel, and ride the "T", the nation's oldest subway system and one of the few to be mentioned in song – *Charlie on the MTA* (Massachusetts Transportation Authority). Also worth your time is a side trip to see **Plymouth Rock, the Mayflower II,** and **Plimoth Plantation**, a "live" museum. Unless you have lots of time, we don't recommend driving to the end of **Cape Cod**, but you might want to try one of the beaches along the way.

Gettysburg (PA) – the best way to absorb the history of this town is to take in one of the shows at the National Park Visitor Center for a general explanation of the sequence of the Civil War battle. Then hire one of the local history buffs (you can make arrangements at the Center) to ride along in your car for a personalized tour of the major battlefields; they know all the details to recreate this event for you.

Hershey (PA)—a chocolate lover's fantasy. The riding tour is fun and you'll learn about the history of chocolate. Be sure to at least splurge on desserts. There is a big amusement park next door, if you wish to incorporate that into your visit. Check out the special lamp posts in town. (717/534-3005)

Lancaster (PA)—the Amish and Mennonite cultures are interesting, but it's difficult to get away from all the commercialism. Sample their cooking at one of the family style restaurants, and tour one of the homes or farms if you want to know more about the simple lifestyle of these plain people. If you're into outlet shopping, you should love the area. Also, there is a great miniature train layout at the Choo Choo Barn in **Strasburg**, and pretzel making (you can actually make one yourself) in **Lititz**, another small town nearby. (717/299-8901)

Mystic Seaport (CT)—restored sea-faring village with many classic ships and boats to explore.

New York City (NY)—Points of interest include: the United Nations building, Lincoln Center, Central Park, Rockefeller Center and other skyscrapers with observation points from upper floors, Ellis Island, and the Statue of Liberty—if you don't have the time to personally visit The Lady, at least observe her as your ancestors might have, by taking the boat trip around Manhattan.

Philadelphia (PA)—see Independence Hall (where the Declaration of Independence was signed), the Liberty Bell, the Betsy Ross House, & various museums. The U.S. Mint has tours.

Stockbridge (MA)—home of Norman Rockwell. If you enjoy his paintings, you might want to visit the museum here.

St. Michaels (MD)—quaint village on the interesting Eastern Shore, where James Michener wrote *Chesapeake*. Visit the Chesapeake Bay Maritime Museum with it's hexagonal lighthouse. (301/745-2916)

Vermont & New Hampshire—picturesque villages and scenic mountain drives.

SOUTHEAST

Atlanta (GA)—get the southern perspective of the Civil War by visiting Stone Mountain Park and Cyclorama at the Civil War Museum. Also of interest: a Coca Cola Museum, Underground Atlanta for shopping, and a nearby Amusement Park.

Charleston (SC)—beautiful antebellum homes in this historical city. (803/353-8000)

Charlotte (NC)—one of the best science museums, Discovery Place, has a 3-story tropical rain forest with live exotic birds & cascading waterfalls. (704/372-6261)

The Kennedy Space Center at Cape Canaveral (FL)–be sure to take the bus tour and see IMAX movie, *The Dream Is Alive,* if you haven't already. It works well to combine this stop with a trip to one of the great beaches along the east coast. (407/452-2121)

Louisville (KY)–home of the famous Churchill Downs Racetrack where the Kentucky Derby horse-race is run annually; many beautiful horse farms in the area.

Nashville (TN)–home of the Grand Ole Opry; there is also a theme park located here.

St. Augustine (FL)–North America's oldest city, the Spanish history is interesting if you have time for this area. Stop at the Information Preview Center near the ancient city gates for an introduction to the city; then walk through the restored district of St. George St., visit the oldest house, and check out Ponce de Leon's Fountain of Youth! Ripley's Believe It or Not Museum is here.

Tampa (FL)–observe animals of Africa roaming in natural surroundings via monorail at Busch Gardens. Kids can ride a camel or an elephant! Other rides available. (813/987-5082)

Williamsburg (VA)–this colonial capital has been handsomely restored; visit homes, craft shops, & exhibition buildings. (804/229-1000)

MIDWEST

Cedar Point (OH)—of many exciting amusement parks around the country, this one is a roller coaster lover's paradise. Located on a peninsula in Lake Erie, one can also choose to take advantage of the beach and related water activities.

Chicago (IL)—take an elevator to the top of the Sears Tower. Visit the Field Museum, Shedd Aquarium, and the Museum of Science & Industry, where you can watch baby chicks hatch and tour a captured German submarine & a replica of a coal mine (312/684–1414). Walk down State St. and check out the beautiful old Palmer House Hotel.

Cincinnati (OH)—has a revitalized downtown with an interconnecting skywalk system, fine museums (including the Taft), and interesting restaurants like eating on a riverboat or in a kiln of a former pottery factory. (800/344–3445)

Fayetteville (WV)—Appalachian Wildwaters operates **white-water raft trips** on the New River (recommended for families) and The Gauley (rougher trips for the more adventurous or older kids). Also in West Virginia are exciting **caving trips**, like Organ Cave at the Lost World Caverns near Lewisburg, where you get to wear the helmets with lights on them. (800/CALL-WVA)

Indianapolis (IN)—home of the famous "Indy 500" auto racetrack; has several museums, including a special one for children.

Milwaukee (WI)—various museums and a lovely zoo; brewery tours.

Shipshewana (IN)— for a look at the Amish culture with less commercialism than Lancaster, PA, you might enjoy this area. There is a wonderful new museum, designed to explain their religion to others, and also several interesting shops. Drive around the area for a look at their farms.

Springfield (IL)—Abraham Lincoln practiced law here; you can tour his home.

St. Louis (MO)—if you're not claustrophobic, the ride inside the arch is an unusual experience. You may also wish to visit the Climatron, a small scale indoor rainforest at the Missouri Botanical Gardens; see rare tropical plants & sparkling waterfalls—learn about ecology.

Toledo (OH)—explore the wilds by visiting the newly revamped Zoological Gardens; the Toledo Museum of Art houses a famed glass collection.

Wisconsin Dells (WI)—famous for boat trips on it's scenic river—fantastic rock forms.

SOUTH

Natchez (MS)—north to Vicksburg for a look at marvelous mansions of the old south—some tours available. (800/647-6742 or 800/647-2290)

New Orleans (LA)—the French influence here is interesting. Try to visit Jackson Square, Preservation Hall (for jazz), a local cemetery (tombs are above ground), sample some cajun food, and treat yourselves to the special doughnuts at Cafe du Monde in the French Quarter on the waterfront. If you really want to splurge, have breakfast at Brennan's! (504/566-5068)

For kids: River Cruise & Audubon Zoo—they have rare white alligators (you can return via streetcar), Pontalba Historical Puppetorium & Louisiana Children's Museum, or **Swamp Tours**, complete with alligators—about 90 minutes west.

NORTHWEST

Alaska—for an introduction to our 50th state take one of the many cruises along the coastline which usually begin in Vancouver and make several stops at rustic towns along the way. The history is fascinating; the scenery spectacular.

Badlands National Park (SD)—not only does this park have a spectacular moonscape of pink & brown banded cliffs, spires, and canyons with fossils, but it also offers the kids plenty of places to run & climb. They'll love the buffalo and prairie dogs—what a combination!

Corn Palace at Mitchell (SD)—this unique building is artistically decorated with various seeds & grasses—located slightly off the main route.

Crater Lake National Park (OR)—one of a kind, the size is impressive, and don't be surprised if you feel a little strange in this eerie place. (503/594-2211)

DeSmet (SD)—visit the home of popular children's author Laura Ingalls Wilder.

Glacier National Park (MT/CAN)—a beautiful area, if it's summertime your family might enjoy hiking to a glacier to play in the snow.

Grand Teton National Park (WY)—jagged mountain peaks make this area unforgetable.

Mount Rushmore (SD)—the giant sculptured faces of Presidents Washington, Jefferson, Lincoln & T. Roosevelt is too famous a landmark to miss! An even larger sculpture, not far away is that of **Crazy Horse**—a memorial to the Indians. Also in the beautiful Black Hills area you can enjoy unusual crossover bridges, the scenic **Needles Highway** with it's towering granite spires, **Custer State Park** with its mountain lakes & ice cold trout streams where the deer and antelope play, and if you go to the town of **Lead,** you can tour the Homestake Gold Mine, the USA's largest!

Wall Drug Store (SD)—the World's Largest Drug Store has an interesting history. Be sure to try their famous buffalo burgers.

WEST

Hearst Castle (CA)—to see this unbelievable estate with it's many art treasures, you are required to take a tour! Get tickets locally at least a day ahead or call in advance. (800/444-PARK).

Los Angeles (CA)—spend a day at **Universal Studios** taking in all of the shows and the tour (try to ride in one of the middle cars for the best special effects). If you or your kids want to be in the Star Trek movie get to that area at least a half hour early. Although you really should see Mann's Chinese Theater and walk the Sidewalk of the Stars, don't expect the **Hollywood** glitz of the past, and try to avoid going there after dark. The once famous Brown Derby is still on the corner of Hollywood & Vine, and if you keep alert, you may see movies or commercials being made anywhere about town. If you want to get tickets to TV shows that are being taped, they are free and are often passed out at Universal Studios, the Chinese Theater, or the Farmers' Market—just hang around or ask someone who looks like they belong. When you do manage to get tickets, plan on spending a lot of time waiting for your show, but it's worth it.

If you really want to see the Homes of the Stars in **Beverly Hills**, try for one of the small tours and hope you get a good driver/guide; be prepared to spend big bucks! Various other tours are also available. Other areas worth seeing are **Venice Muscle Beach** (most interesting for far out people-watching on a weekend), the LaBrea Tar Pits for fossils, Rodeo Drive for shopping (window-shopping is probably all you can afford here, but you might see someone famous), and the city of **Long Beach**, where you can tour the famous "flying" Spruce Goose and the Queen Mary, where you just may be able to get your picture taken with Clark Gable, Mae West, or other famous stars from the past. You might also want to include **Disneyland** and/ or **Knott's Berry Farm.**

Redwood and/or Sequoia National Parks (CA)— seeing is believing! To fully appreciate the magnitude of these rare trees, hike some of the trails and read about their history in one of several museums located in the parks. There are also smaller State Parks which serve the same purpose, and may be more convenient for your trip. (209/565-3341).

San Francisco (CA)—interesting highlights: Pier 39 & Fisherman's Wharf, a cable car ride, Lombard St., Chinatown, the Golden Gate Bridge, Nob Hill and shopping at Ghirardelli Square (be sure to buy a few chocolate samples). The Exploratorium Science Museum has a tactile dome & wave organ (415/561–0360). If you have time, you may want to take the boat trip for a tour of the former Alcatraz Prison.

Yosemite National Park (CA)—for breathtakingly beautiful mountain scenery, this area can't be beat!

SOUTHWEST

Bryce & Zion National Parks (801/772–3256) (UT)—colorful canyons, impressive formations, & landscapes. Hiking & trail rides.

Carlsbad Caverns National Park (NM)—the largest underground chambers yet discovered. If that's too out of the way, visit one of the smaller but still interesting caves, such as Mammoth Cave (KY) or Organ Cave (WV).

Denver (CO)—U.S. Mint, Art Museum, and Larimer Square for Victorian buildings, shops, & galleries. Side trips available: **Railroad Museum, Central Gold Mine, & Coors Brewery.**

Four Corners (AZ,UT,CO,NM)—the only place you can be in four states at the same time—be sure to have your picture taken. As this is Indian Territory, you will be touched by the conditions by which many of them have to live—look for their traditional round homes, called hogans. Be sure to visit **Monument Valley** & the dinosaur tracks west of **Tuba City.**

Hoover Dam (NV)—the size is impressive, finding a place to park can be a problem.

Las Vegas (NV)—seeing is believing! Even if you don't want to risk your money in the casinos, you can't lose on the low price of meals and hotel accommodations. We understand the new Excalibur has a great roller coaster & also a very exciting train ride. For recorded information about shows, hotels, & area attractions call 702/457-4664 or write them (2301 E. Sahara Ave. Las Vegas NV 89104).

Monument Valley (UT/AZ)—this remote area, which features mesas, buttes, cliffs, canyons, monoliths, and other unique sandstone geological attractions, is part of the Navejo Indian Reservation. Many TV commercials are filmed here.

Petrified Forest National Park (AZ)—petrified logs up to 100 feet long lie in the Rainbow Forest.

Pike's Peak (CO)—for a spectacular view, ride the Cog Railroad to the summit.

Salt Lake City (UT)—Mormon center and home of the famous Tabernacle Choir. Nearby is The Great Salt Lake, where one could easily float in the heavy salt water.

HAWAII (800/923–1811)

Although becoming heavily commercialized, there are still areas where you can feel the harmony & blending of many races & cultures like nowhere else in the world. If possible, visit the island of **Oahu** to see Diamond Head & Waikiki Beach (You can hike to the rim for an impressive view of the Waikiki Skyline), Pearl Harbor & Punch Bowl Cemetery, the magnificent Iolani Palace, the Polynesian Cultural Center, and if you can, see the Kodak Hula Show, tour a pineapple factory, visit Sea Life Park, Blow Hole, & The Pali (cliff), and shop at the International Marketplace.

Kauai has Waimea Canyon, Kalelau Lookout, and The Fern Grotto. On **Maui** visit the old whaling village of Lahaina (check out the islands' largest Banyan Tree behind the courthouse), the Iao Needle, and if time, there are many parks, waterfalls, & gardens to explore. On The Big Island, **Hawaii**, you'll find Honaunau National Historic Park and Hawaii Volcanoes National Park, lava flows, steam cracks, sulphur banks, and black sand beaches.

In general, take advantage of the many hiking opportunites, look for orchid, pineapple, & sugar cane fields, try the Kona coffee, teriyaki steak, and/or mahi mahi (dolphin fish), and take a hula lesson at your hotel! If you wish to attend a luau, you will need a reservation – inquire as to where they are being held in advance, through your hotel. (Some State Parks have inexpensive bungalows to rent – reserve early 808/335-6061)

CANADA

Edmonton (AL)—is the home of the world's Largest Mall which features not only 800 stores & services, but also a Fantasyland Theme Park, a world Water Park with the world's largest wave pool, an ice skating rink, mini-golf, submarine rides, and more. Family passes available. (800/661-8890)

Montreal (QU)—you will enjoy the French flavor of the city; eat at one of the outdoor cafes. The Old Montreal Walking Tour includes some of the same cobblestone paths that were used by the fur traders & missionaries. Bonsecours, the "sailors" church, has boat shaped chandeliers, and a favorite of kids is it's historical museum in the basement with doll size figures. Try to visit the Notre Dame Cathedral when the organ is being played— impressive!

Stratford (ON)—this charming town on the banks of the Avon River is famous for Shakespeare and other productions on it's Festival Stage. (519/271-4040)

Toronto (ON)—a great place for kids! There is the Ontario Science Center (a wonderful hands-on science museum), a real castle like some in Europe (they'll love climbing Casa Loma's towers), Ontario Place with it's Children's Village (an amazing assortment of water & other fun activities for kids), a very good subway system, great shopping centers like The Eaton Center, interesting buildings (check out some of the lobbies with atriums), and unusual places to eat—like The Spaghetti Factory and many ethnic restaurants.

ADD-ONS

ADD-ONS

BEST KEPT SECRETS

Devil's Tower National Monument (WY)—this monolith, a one of a kind natural landmark, is actually the core of an ancient volcano—awesome! Also, prairie dogs.

Mesa Verde (CO)—climb into the past by exploring the cliff dwellings of these ancient peoples (the Anasazi)—truly fascinating! Don't miss the small but excellent museum.

Falling Water (PA)—this unique Frank Lloyd Wright house is built over a waterfall.

The House on the Rock, west of Madison (WI)—this extraordinary multi-level home stands atop a chimney-like rock overlooking the Wyoming Valley; massive fireplaces, pools of running water, & waterfalls add to it's uniqueness. Many interesting exhibits, including: dolls, a miniature village with animated people, carrousels, circus items, theater organs, and shops.

Library of Congress Building (DC)—the beautiful interior decor is rare in this country; Lincoln's drafts of his *Gettysburg Address* are here.

Riverhouse Resort in Bend (OR)—if you have time, splurge on a night at this picturesque resort. Built around a rocky stream, enjoy the different pools & hot tubs.

Michigan Highlights—We're proud of our home state! (Travel Bureau 800/5432-YES)

Detroit—see the famous Renaissance Center on the river (a city within a city), include a ride on the People Mover to Greek Town for shopping and dinner, and if you can afford tickets, go to the Fox Theater—the huge, recently renovated theater with it's ornate decor is like buildings usually seen only in Europe—Awesome! (Drive or take a cab) Nearby in **Dearborn** is Henry Ford's Greenfield Village, where it's many carefully restored buildings give us vivid glimpses of early America, including the history of the automobile at the museum next door. Also in the area, you can tour his mansion and those of other auto magnates, especially in Grosse Pointe Shores & Rochester. Kids will enjoy taking the boat to the Boblo Island Amusement Park.

Flint (800/482-6708) has Crossroads Village, a living museum and sort of mini version of Greenfield Village but less $ – our kids loved trying the stilts and playing with other old fashioned toys, the train ride was fun, and we saw a great magic show. The Sloan Museum in town is a good one.

Lansing's capitol building, which is currently being restored to its original splendor, has many unusual artistic features such as it's glass floor in the rotunda, symbolic copper chandeliers, and massive carved wooden doors (tours available). Close by is the unique Michigan Historical Museum and the Impression Five Science Museum, with exciting hands-on experiences for children.

Other interesting cities are: **Grand Haven**—it has a lighted Musical Fountain that performs daily at dusk during the summer and at tulip time (You might want to check with the Chamber of Commerce), and great beaches. For an ethnic experience visit the most popular tourist attraction in Michigan, **Frankenmuth**, with it's Bavarian charm, covered bridge, quaint shops, famous Christmas store (Bronner's), and restaurants (Zehnder's or the Bavarian Inn). Or for a Dutch treat go to **Holland** to see wooden shoes being carved, DeZwann—the only authentic Dutch windmill in this country, and the Dutch Village—in the spring you'll enjoy the vast fields of tulips, in summer you can cool off at one of the sandy beaches of close-by Lake Michigan. **Ann Arbor** hosts one of the largest art fairs in the U.S. annually during July, with artists participating from most of the states. (313/995-7281). You'll also want to try some of the wide variety of ethnic restaurants. Nearby Dominos Farms is World Headquarters for Dominos Pizza; it offers a Frank Lloyd Wright Museum, a classic car collection, and a petting zoo—something for everyone!

Popular tourist spots in beautiful **Northern Lower Michigan** include: Sleeping Bear National Lakeshore—you won't believe the size of these mountains of sand, the whole family will love climbing & playing on them; The Platte River for floating and canoeing, with interesting fish hatchery nearby; poet & artist Gwen Frostic's home and print shop, shows nature at it's best—delightful and interesting for both kids & adults (Benzonia). Traverse City has Tall Ship Cruises or stay on one as a Bed & Breakfast (616/941–2000); also at Northport (800/678–0383) & Charlevoix. For culture, visit the National Music Camp at Interlochen and enjoy superb performances of all of the arts in natural surroundings every night except Mondays. Horton Bay on Lake Charlevoix is Ernest Hemingway country—check out the general store.

Beaver Island, 32 miles out from the beautiful resort town of Charlevoix, was at one time a Mormon Colony, ruled by a king—island tours are sometimes available. Even more remote are the Islands of Manitou (616/256–9061) and Isle Royale (906/289–4437).

In the **Upper Peninsula** visit Sault Ste. Marie (take the boat trip to see how the Soo Locks work—interesting, but long), The Old Indian Burial Grounds with graves protected by traditional wooden shelters (Brimley), the picturesque Tahquemenon Falls, the Fayettville Ghost Town, and the Pictured Rocks National Lakeshore at Munising (906/387–2379), made famous by Longfellow's poem "Hiawatha"—visit by cruise boat from the Municipal Pier.

* **NOTE**—There are also many excellent theme parks and attractions for families: such as Sea World & Marineland, amusement parks, water parks, various boat charters, and if you have older kids, white water rafting with several locations around the country. So keep this in mind as you plan your future trips. If you

have an extra day available, these make great fillers and a nice break from an educational vacation.

Tips for Crowded Tourist Attractions:

* **Get a map ahead and plan your order of attack—if possible, start at the back & work your way to the front.**

* **Wear matching bright colored or identical striped shirts.**

* **Always have a meeting place in case someone gets lost.**

ADD-ONS

ADD-ONS

MAJOR DISAPPOINTMENTS

It's possible that these places may have changed if you want to take a chance, but at the time of our visits, they ranked at the top of our Major Disappointments List.

Cave of the Winds (CO)—we thought it looked artificial because they have painted various areas inside the cave.

China Court (Toronto)—we walked a long way to get there, and found very little when we did.

Circus Circus (Las Vegas)—prices are good, but if you think you'll see a lot of circus acts, you'll be disappointed. They are few and far between. It seems like the main idea is to get your kids to blow their money at the arcade while they are waiting!

CN Tower (Toronto)—waited close to 2 hours in line (although we haven't heard of anyone else waiting this long) for an overpriced tour which included listening to an unintelligible narrative on ear phones.

As it turns out this is an amazingly short list, when you consider the amount of traveling we've done. So it would appear that either we are easy to please (those who know us would never believe it), or our advance planning paid off!

ADD-ONS

CHAPTER 6
OTHER WAYS TO GO
A Better Idea?

Although the main focus of this book deals with leaving the driving to you, I realize that in this fast paced world in which we live, driving your own vehicle sometimes is not the best way to go, especially with current environmental concerns (fuel consumption, air pollution, etc.) However, I do feel that the only way to really appreciate and understand the vastness and beauty of our country is to at some point in time, drive across as much of it as you can. To be able to share this experience with your children is a wonderful gift, a great way to bring their education to life! I also feel strongly that we should have an awareness of our own country before we can be good representatives elsewhere.

As mentioned before, there are some times when other options make more sense; not only the time element, but also from an educational perspective. Some of the secondary benefits of not driving include: learning to be organized, keeping on a schedule, not taking it all with you (living with less), being adaptable, meeting other people, and of course, how to use public transportation (surviving without a car). Many of these lessons will prove to be valuable throughout the lives of both you and your children. Let's take a brief look at these other choices.

PLANE

If you are really short on time, this mode of travel becomes the obvious choice, especially if your mind is set on a particular destination that is not very close to home. However, if time is really not a problem and you don't have important stops you need to make along the route, you should still look into some of the many airline discounts. Although some of the best deals, such as last minute stand-bys, are not very suitable for families and people who need to plan ahead, there are other discount plans available, such as: super-saver, frequent flyer, kid discounts, early bookings, night flights, midweek travel, or lower rates due to airfare wars. You also might want to consider a tour package which includes airfare. Check newspapers for specials, or call an agent, your travel club, or the airlines (most have toll free numbers). After investigating, you may find that you will actually save money by paying what may seem like a lot for airfare, when you compare it to the totals that you would have to pay for having to spend several days on the road—food, gas, and lodging. Not only that, unless you run into problems, you will arrive at your vacation spot, more relaxed and ready to enjoy!

If you are considering this route, keep in mind available transportation from the airport, when choosing your hotel. Find out if they have a courtesy van; otherwise, take into account the costs of other methods such as cabs, airport shuttles, or public transportation—although a bus may not be an option if you have a lot of luggage. Or, if you will need to be doing a lot of coming and going to places off the beaten path, you may choose to rent a car. As with everything else, you should call ahead of time to make sure one to your liking will be available (most car rental companies also have toll free numbers).

TIPS

* **Always carry a bag with you on the plane with all your valuables, and also have your essentials for at least one day.**

* **Call the airline or your travel agent ahead of time so that you can reserve the popular window seats for your kids; also plan to arrive at the airport early and check in at the boarding gate—the airlines do overbook, and you don't want to be left behind.**
* **Keep your baggage claim check—it's your only proof that you checked your bags.**
* **You can request special meals; agents can usually show you meal choices—allow at least 48 hours in advance.**
* **Report any problem to the airline representative before you leave the airport.**

TRAIN

This travel option is an exciting one for kids. Instead of being belted into a car or plane seat for hours at a time, they can actually explore the whole train by going from one car to another. Amtrak offers a variety of accommodations and facilities depending upon what section of the country you plan to travel, and kids age 2–15 ride for half price! Reservations are needed for long distance trips and for sleeping accommodations. Group plans and package tours are available such as AIR/RAIL or AIR/SAIL, which open up limitless choices and avoid the possibility of having to backtrack. For example: You can take the train to your destination, but fly back, without being penalized by having to buy two one-way tickets.

Many people have enjoyed the scenic cross-Canada route, or you can do just part of it, enjoying the interesting cities of a particular area. Conrail passes save money on unlimited travel throughout the system and are good for 1 month. With the All Aboard America Plan, you have 45 days for a round trip across the United States choosing a different return route if you like, and making any three stops you wish at no extra charge. An option for those wishing to have their car in Florida and not eager to drive the whole way, is to take the Auto Train from near Washington, D.C. to Sanford in Central Florida. (800/USA RAIL or VIA Rail Canada at 800/387-1144)

Those who prefer having their itineraries taken care of by someone else, should look into the many complete tours (including Canada & Mexico) offered by America by Rail. (800/351-7411)

BOAT

Size and types of cruises are limitless, including a wide variety of facilities, activities, and events—even Theme Cruises. Most must be booked through a travel agent, who can help you find one that best meets your needs and advise you on what you will need to take. As with the airlines the best deals are available for early bookings or last minute availability.

There are also several River Boat Cruises available from companies such as Steamboatin' on the Mississippi & Ohio Rivers, Mississippi River Cruises (800/

331–1467), and the Delta Queen Steamboat Company (800/543–1949).

If you're looking for a little more boating excitement, you might want to consider using your vacation to learn a new skill—sailing! Several sailing schools are available, including: Annapolis (800/638–9192), in New York (800/221–4326), in Rhode Island (800/343–2255), and in San Diego (800/666–1050). Or try one of the Windjammer Barefoot Cruises—in Florida (800/327–2601).

BUS

Often the lowest priced transportation available, buses can get to many towns where other forms of transportation don't go, with unlimited stopover privileges. Tours range from one day excursions to month long transcontinental tours. Major companies offer unlimited travel passes. Often special discounts are available on hotels & tourist attractions. Call or write the major motor coach line in your area. Ask about special fares or charter package tours. Many package tours are also available through travel clubs or organizations in your community. Check newspapers and community education brochures.

TIPS

* **Long distance bus travel can be monotonous and tiring, so if possible, plan stopovers at interesting places.**

* **If checking bags, try to make sure you see them loaded into the luggage compartment before boarding.**

AUTO & RV RENTAL

For information, check the yellow pages of your phone book for local dealers (for RV's check under Campers or Motor Homes). Be sure to ask for all the charges before renting—your insurance, mileage costs, etc. Check your auto insurance policy or call your insurance agent to determine whether you will need to buy the extra insurance (not cheap) that the car rental agency is eager to add on to your daily rental cost. Also check on who is allowed to drive—some companies may charge extra for additional drivers. For information about traveling with a group of RV's, look under Caravans at the end of this chapter.

COVERED WAGON

For a taste of the pioneer spirit, your family might want to try one of several 2–6 day wagon treks. In Wyoming you can call 307/886-5240 or 307/733-5386; in Nevada (308/586-1850) or Kansas (316/321-6300). For a 1 day adventure in Arizona (602/977-7724) or Kansas (316/321-6300).

LOCAL: Bus, Cab, Subway, Cable Car, Water Taxi

Be sure to investigate this when booking a hotel in a city (you can always get the details after you arrive). Even if you're traveling by car, many times it's more convenient and less expensive to use public transportation for coming & going to city attractions, and leave your car at the hotel. For example, fine subway systems in places like Washington, D.C. and Toronto are fast and new experiences for kids.

WHEN TO USE A TRAVEL AGENT

If you have decided that one of these other transportation options is the most appropriate for the trip you are planning, a Travel Agency can be invaluable. Travel agents have at their fingertips more information, more than we can ever obtain on our own. With a minimum of time and effort they can put together a trip that's tailor made to your family's needs, and budget. They can arrange appropriate connections, rentals, accommodations, tours, combinations (AIR/RAIL) packages, etc. plus furnish you with a wealth of useful information from tipping tips to what kind of weather to expect. All this, usually is at no charge, because costs are covered by their suppliers. However, travel agents do vary in knowledge, experience, and integrity; so be selective. Get recommendations from friends or make sure the agent has a membership in the American Society of Travel Agents. We contacted several agents before choosing a really good one to plan a cruise.

DISCOUNT TRAVEL AGENTS & TRAVEL CLUBS

Most of these companies deal with last minute bookings; if that is an option for you, you may locate them by looking in ads of the Travel section of your local paper, but be cautious about what you will actually be getting for your money.

PACKAGE DEALS & CHARTERS

For package deals and charters, look for lowest fare specialists, also in the ads in the Travel section of your newspaper. Tour companies operate by getting a bulk rate, then passing the savings along to you.

A Final Thought

Generally speaking, cutting costs with these other modes of transportation, usually involves time, effort, inconvenience, or discomfort—in other words trade-offs. The more flexible you can be, the better your chances of saving. Remember, however, in planning for your trips that a budget means sensible spending, not cheap! One reason some people prefer package tours or resort vacations is that they know and pay for costs in advance, so they don't have to worry about budgeting. All arrangements are made for you, so you are free to relax and enjoy your trip (what, me worry!)—you can even find tour packages geared for people with common interests. But one of the disadvantages of these vacations, is that you lose a lot of your flexibility.

PHONE NUMBERS & OTHER HELPFUL INFORMATION

Airlines—check the front of your phone book or call the 800 information number.

America By Rail—many tours to choose from in the U.S., Canada, & Mexico. Golden Spike Deluxe & Railblazer Class offer first class hotels, extensive sightseeing, & many meals. (800/351-7411)

American Automobile Association (AAA)—membership will make available travel planning, tours, and many discounts. They are very good about sending you excellent information upon request. (800/482-5300) or call locally as listed in your phone book.

American Association of Retired Persons (AARP)—If over age 50, a membership provides travel discounts.

American Bed & Breakfast Association—804/379-2222 for annual directory of Bed & Breakfasts; check your local libraries & bookstores for guidebooks. When calling B & B's be sure to ask if they take kids.

American Express—800/843-2273 to apply, or see phone book for other credit card companies. If you join their Travel Club (annual fee), you can get 10-50 percent savings on some air fares, hotels, & rental cars. Departure from major cities only. (800/421-8758)

American Youth Hostels—national office (202/783-6161) or write P.O. Box 37613, Department USA, Washington D.C. 20013-7613 for information—overnight fees range from $5.-$13.

Amtrak—escorted full service train tours—especially in the west and combination deals with plane, cruise ship, etc. Kids 2-15 half price (800/USA-RAIL) or in Canada. (800/387-1144)

Association of Elder Hostels—educational opportunities at many colleges & universities for older adults; catalogs available at your local library, call 617/426-8056, or write 75 Federal St., Boston, MA 02110 or P.O. Box 1959, Wakefield MA, 01880-5959.

Buses—call individual companies as listed in the 800 number listings in the front of your local phone book; check local community education, colleges, & travel agencies & clubs for bus trips.

Caravan Trips for RV's—for information on the options & extras available by traveling in a group, call Trails-a-way in MI (800/346-7572), Creative World Rallies & Caravans in LA (800/732-8337) or contact the Recreation Vehicle Industry Assn. (P.O. Box 2999) Dept. RK, Reston, VA 22090.

Chamber of Commerce—call information for a particular city, or write.

Colleges & Universities—call information for a particular college, OR write Campus Travel Service for their Travel Accommodations Guide, which offers rooms for vacationing families at 340 universities in 30 nations. Cost $13. Address: P.O. Box 8355, Newport Beach, CA 92660.

Condo Network—800/874-1411

Convention & Visitors Association (Washington D.C.) 202/737-8866

Cruise Lines—see 800 listings in front of local phone book; however, it's best to contact a travel agent.

Fraternities & Sororities—if you are a member of one, you may be able to stay at some of their houses, if space permits; call information for a particular university location. (this idea is best for single travelers)

Home Exchange—look in the library for a home exchange clearinghouse which publishes annual directories of people interested in swapping houses (if you plan to do this, be sure to get references).

Lighthouses—Big Bay Point in Michigan's Upper Peninsula is the only Bed & Breakfast in the U.S. to be located in a lighthouse! (906/345-9957). Full service Inns are located in San Francisco and in Maine at Isle au Haut.

KOA cabins—406/248-7444 or send $3. to KOA, P.O.Box 30558, Billings, MT. 19114 for a National Directory.

Lodging Discounts—*The Travel America at Half Price Book* ($26.95). Call 800/521-9640.

Motel Chains—major ones should be listed under the 800 numbers in the front of your local phone book.

Mississippi River Cruises—2 day river cruises. (800/331-1467, in IL 800/237-1660)

Mobil Travel Guide—guidebooks list motels & restaurants for various parts of the country; available at libraries & bookstores—lists 800 numbers. Discount coupons.

National Park Service—202/208-4747

Rent-a-Car—major ones should be listed with the 800 numbers in the front of your local phone book.

Rental Condos—locate through travel agents, airlines, or classified ads.

Steamboatin'—Mississippi & Ohio River Paddle Wheel steamboat vacations (800/543-1949)

Steam Passenger Service Directory—for a full list of tourist railroads & railroad museums (over 263 in the USA), call 800/356-0246.

Travel Agencies—see local phone book.

Travel Coupons & Discount Cards—discounts on hotels & restaurants. Some people have been happy with the coupon books from Entertainment Publications (313/637-8400) or ask a travel agent.

Travel or Tourist Bureaus—Call information (800/555-1212) and ask for a particular state.

TWA Travel Club—save up to 30% of lowest published fare on short-notice departures. Annual fee. (800/872-8364)

U.S. Chamber of Commerce—(202/659-6000)

Washington D.C. Central Reservation Center— will actually match you to a particular hotel according to your budget. (800/554-2220)

Windjammer Barefoot Cruises—adventure sailing cruises in the Caribbean. (800/327-2601)

Western Union—can transfer emergency money by phone or wire. (800/325-6000)

YMCA—call information for a particular city; ask about Y's Way International or general accommodations.

TO GET A SPECIFIC PHONE NUMBER

Call 1-800-555-1212 to see if there is an 800 number. If not, call 1 (area code) 555-1212—check your phone book for the correct area code or call your local information number to get it.

* Note—All numbers cannot be reached from all locations

INDEX

Happy Traveling!

A GREAT GIFT IDEA

Additional copies of LUXURY TRAVEL FOR THE UNRICH AND UNFAMOUS by Beth Hubbell are available at many bookstores or use the convenient order form below— $7.95 each.

Please send _______ copies of *LUXURY TRAVEL FOR THE UNRICH AND UNFAMOUS by Beth Hubbell* to the following address:

Name ____

Address ____

City ____________State ____________Zip Code ___________

Sales tax:
Please add 4% for books shipped to Michigan addresses.

Shipping:
Book Rate: $1.50 for the first book and 50 cents for each additional copy.

Payment: check or money order

Enclosed is my Total Payment of _________ which includes the cost of books, tax if applicable, and shipping charges. If not completely satisfied, books may be returned for a full refund.

Mail order to:
Jeremiah Publications
1158 Woodside Dr. #102
Haslett, MI 48840

Shipped within 1 week upon receipt of orders.